Flowers *of a* Moment

버려야 할 것이

흘러가는 때 꽃닢

2 꽃

Flowers *of a* Moment

Poems by Ko Un

Translated by Brother Anthony of Taizé,
Young-moo Kim, and Gary Gach

BOA Editions, Ltd.   ℮   Rochester, NY   ☺   2006

First Edition
06 07 08 09 7 6 5 4 3 2 1

Publications by BOA Editions, Ltd.—a not-for-profit corporation under section 501 (c) (3) of the United States Internal Revenue Code—are made possible with the assistance of grants from the Literature Program of the New York State Council on the Arts; the Literature Program of the National Endowment for the Arts; the County of Monroe, NY; the Lannan Foundation for support of the Lannan Translations Selection Series; the Sonia Raiziss Giop Charitable Foundation; the Mary S. Mulligan Charitable Trust; the Rochester Area Community Foundation; the Arts & Cultural Council for Greater Rochester; the Steeple-Jack Fund; the Elizabeth F. Cheney Foundation; the Chesonis Family Foundation; the Ames-Amzalak Memorial Trust in memory of Henry Ames, Semon Amzalak and Dan Amzalak; and contributions from many individuals nationwide.

Cover Design: Steve Smock
Cover Painting: Brush drawing by Ko Un
Interior Design and Composition: Richard Foerster
Manufacturing: McNaughton & Gunn, Lithographers
BOA Logo: Mirko

Library of Congress Cataloging-in-Publication Data

Ko, Un, 1933–
   [Sun'gan ui kkot. English]
   Flowers of a moment / by Ko Un ; translated by Brother Anthony, Young-moo Kim, and Gary Gach. — 1st American ed.
      p. cm. — (Lannan translations selection series)
      ISBN 1–929918–87–9 (hardcover : alk. paper) — ISBN 1–929918–88–7 (pbk. : alk. paper)
      I. Anthony, of Taizé, Brother, 1942– II. Kim, Young-mu, 1944– III. Gach, Gary. IV. Title. V. Series.

PL992.42.U5s8613 2006
895.7'14—dc22

2006007143

Contents

Author's Preface

I really don't know why, but tonight is still, so very still.

It is so still I can almost hear the wind-borne sand singing on the slopes of Mount Mingsha in Dunhuang, far away on the Silk Road, penetrating all this way.

Thousands of quiet miles!

Might that be the sound of the void summoning the void, of names summoning names? That still sound of someone advancing along the road that lies beyond good and evil, the sound of that soundlessness which we call the stillness that is Nirvana. The sound of the empty circle, after the beautiful and the ugly, good and bad, and all such-like, are transcended, or rather at the state where even that sound has vanished.

Here am I, daring to upset such stillness.

Perhaps the world's very first question was, "What is a poem?" Might that be why, at critical moments throughout the ages, this question "What is a poem?" never fails to repeat itself?

Sixty thousand years ago, the Neanderthal people, burying their dead, decorated a bier with green branches, purple hyacinths, yellow crown-daisies, hollyhocks, yarrow, etc. and laid the body on it. This was discovered in the Shanidar Cave in Iraq. The body of a boy from the Paleolithic Age, some twenty thousand years ago, was discovered in a cave in Korea's North Chungcheong Province, with fossilized chrysanthemums on his brow. Likewise in Egypt, a wreath of flowers was found on the head of the boy pharaoh Tutankhamen, who died three thousand three hundred years ago.

I am convinced this heart-offering of flowers is the essence of poetry. The poetics and poetic theories that evolved in East and West since classical times are, most likely, much later developments. Long before, people prayed with poetic hearts for their dead to be reborn in another world, a world of flowers, flowers representing the sorrow arising between presence and absence.

And as poetry has accompanied humanity through tens of thousands of years, it has become the very essence of that vast time span. A single line of poetry—a single word, even—can yolk me to ten thousand aeons.

Poetry is, inevitably, a pledge made to the future. And so eternal essence manifests itself as dream. Thus, there are as many different dreams as people.

I find myself fascinated by the spiritual traces left by former poets. The dreams of former poets are illuminating. Some poets' vocations begin in their dreams.

One poet is said to have borrowed five writing brushes of different colors from a dream and wrote poems with them. Then, having restored the brush to its owner in his dream, poems no longer came to him. Left poemless, he could no longer find any reason to go on living, so he quit this world.

Another poet too began through dreams. In a dream, he vomited a dazzling double-tailed phoenix from his mouth; it flew aloft and from the next day onward an abundance of poems began to arise on wings of their own.

Another poet, too, began life as a poet by dreaming. Once, a peony blossomed at the tip of a brush in his dream; then, between dreaming and waking, he'd write ten thousand poems that would cause all the spirits in and beneath the heavens to weep. It was not only a matter of poems; he is also said to have drunk ten thousand cups of wine while he wrote those poems. In life, he was the world; in death, the cosmos.

Yet another poet began with a dream. On rough, rocky slopes, grass could only be found very high up. A shepherd with his flock of sheep had nearly reached the summit of such a mountain. As he gazed down at the world spread below, that shepherd was overpowered with sleep.

He dreamed. Nine nymphs appeared in his dream. He awoke. It was his real life, and the nine nymphs were still there with him. In a voice clear as jade ringing in the pellucid air, one of them spoke: "Henceforth, you are a poet. A poet who will sing all the truth of the world."

Thus, an utterly illiterate shepherd, who had no idea what a poem was, began the life of a poet. From him streamed a continual fountain of poems. Though poems are written down, those poems were not manufactured; they came to birth on their own.

Might all the dreams of those poets also be mine, dreamed by me, in this and in other worlds as well?

A certain number of my poems have been composed in dreams. Just last night a poem arose in my dreams — not so much a poem composed by me as a poem given to me by someone else. That someone else may have been myself in a previous existence. Or it might have been the self I shall become in a future world.

Here's the poem:

Offer your whole wretched life to darkness.
You speckled
speeding waves
strike break smash
against the cliffs in the dark.
Light will be born. Day will dawn.

Recalling the poem upon waking, it is utterly unfamiliar. Some dream poems are very long and so vanish completely once I awake, but mostly they are like this one, only not so long. My brief poems have their roots in my dreams.

Imagine a poet composing poems while riding on a donkey's back. Sometimes when he coughs, even his spit will become a poem. Some poets have said they drink poetry. Someone once said I breathe poetry.

A drifting cloud has paused along its way.

On a moonlit night, the whole wide world for hundreds of miles around forms one household. On such a moonlit night, if you recite a poem then play the flute, the moon will pause in its course through the heavens and stay for a long while listening to poems from earth.

Is this only heaven's concern? How could it be only a matter of heaven's sun, moon, stars? Poems used to curl round the rafters of Korean houses, reverberating far and wide. Poetry was first in the heavens, then came down to earth. So the poet, likewise, having fled or been exiled from heaven, has received an earthly destiny.

Certainly, this isn't without painful inner conflict, with such questions as "What is poetry in the face of aggression, oppression, and poverty? " and "What is poetry in a world full of greed, ignorance, and disease?" Even faced with the challenge of whether writing poetry might be at all possible after Auschwitz, poetry has remained unbowed. I began to write my first poems as if they were tufts of grass among the ruins left by the Korean War, where up to four million perished.

The ancient Korean Buddhist monk Wonhyo combined the truth dependent on words with the truth that is wordless. Here is the possibility of poetry entering a state that mysteriously transcends the limits of narrative.

Buddhist Soen meditation is a negation of words and writing. Yet, upon attaining its goal, word-flowers blossom, paradoxically.

I have written lengthy poems; long, long poems; and several epics. Opposite are these flowers of a moment.

be on your way.
you are the very first, and next after the very first.
go on and on.
viewed in reverse, you are advancing
quickly
baby tongue of a spring narcissus in a snowstorm.

Ko Un

At sunset

a wish:
to become a wolf beneath a fat full moon

      *

I have spent the whole day talking about other people again
and the trees are watching me
as I go home

      *

Exhausted
the mother has fallen asleep
so her baby is listening all alone
to the sound of the night train

One rainy spring day
I looked out once or twice
wondering if someone would be coming by

*

Wings on one side torn off
a fly crawls awkwardly away

Today's come to an end

*

Lingering winter snow is a holy thing
Larch trees
all bare of leaves
stand hesitating
hesitating
never lying—by not even a single word

I boldly go on past this place

In Mount Kariwang in Chongson, Kangwon Province
the falling streams
are busy but busier are
the minnows, the carplings
swimming upwards
against the current

*

If I lie down, I'll be done for
an ailing animal
desperately
staying standing all day long

It's been that kind of day in the world, my dear

A mother giraffe
considerately shares its milk
with other mothers' babes

Little Sunchol's mother gazes into the distance
as she offers her cold breast to motherless Hongil's younger brother

*

The night bird sings with all its might
while the stars are shining with all their might
In a world like this I lie down confidently
and bid sleep come

*

April 19
The first snake of spring emerged
and died!

I have lived too long!

Never sad
Never troubled
Is that why
there's a newly born smile?

A new-born baby's sleeping face

*

Rowing with just one oar
I lost that oar

For the first time I looked round at the wide stretch of water

At the table next to mine
there's talk of how much they earned today
of one thing and another

those two young men
drinking *soju*
are already husbands and fathers

*

Outside the cave the howling wind and rain
Inside
the silent speech of bats filling the ceiling

*

April 30
Look at that pale green hue on So-un Mountain

On such a day
what love
what hate

Summer vacation—the primary school classrooms are quiet
In one classroom
there's a harmonium where
the Fa in the scale is dead
In that classrom is the framed
national flag they hung there forty-two years ago
and in that classroom
remain
the daring graffiti of times gone by

"Kim Ok-ja has the biggest boobs"

*

Two beggars
sharing a meal of the food they've been given

The new moon shines intensely

In the very middle of the road
two dogs are coupling

I take another route

                    *

                    A photo studio's shop window
                    A woman who cannot bear children
                    gazes smiling at a photo of a one-year-old child

                    *

                              Straighten your clothes!
                              In a blazing kiln
                              a pot is being fired

"I've come, dear
The harsh winter's over now"

His wife's tomb laughs quietly

*

Some say they can recall a thousand years
Some say they have already visited the next thousand years
On a windy day
I am waiting for a bus

*

What do you think you're doing landing like that
on the back of my hand as I'm writing a letter to my daughter?
First visitor of this year's spring
you yellow butterfly

We went to Auschwitz
saw the mounds of glasses
saw the piles of shoes
On the way back
we each stared out of a different window

*

A baby dragonfly perches on a bulrush tip
The entire world surrounds it, watching

*

Beneath the heavens with their scattered clouds
here and there are fools

Crayfish, why are you so complicated?

with your feelers
your jaw legs
your hairy legs
your chest legs
your belly legs
and all the rest

*

When all's said and done
the lake
is still where it was
after bidding someone goodbye

*

In a poor family's yard
the moon's so bright it could beat out rice-cakes

Hey, May beetle
shaking your wings
even you are singing

                    *

                    Be like a dandelion seed
                    floating in the breeze
                    Be like a bearded late autumn reed seed

                    Set out alone, create a great new world

                              *

                              Look, that dandelion drenched by a shower
                              is making the best of it, pursing its lips

                              Stand firm, little girl

26

In the garden, snow is falling
Inside, no one realizes

*

Following the tracks of an animal in the snow
I looked back at my own tracks

*

That cicada's cry!
emerging after
ten or fifteen years underground
We should all be grateful

Beneath the blue sky
there's a baby in a womb

                    *

                        Up
                        there on the Changtang Plateau
                        of Tibet
                                in Ali
                        inhabited by humans
                        kids
                        fighting were watched by
                        a dog who lifting his leg
                        pissed
                        for some time.

                    *

This is my native village, as it was before

They say Sunam is dead—
as a kid he was good at catching crayfish
and Sangmun, who used help Sunam
turn over the stones
where the crayfish were hiding
is dead
and at the mill Kyongho is dead too

Once the snow has melted,
the barley fields stay green a long while

       *

Two people are eating
facing each other

The most routine thing
and at the same time
the best thing

Like they say, it's love

In my dreams last night
two lines of a poem came to me
but on waking up
I lost one

雪月三更無餘句라

Moonlight
on snow
Bright midnight
No more words remain

　　　　*

Every worm
grows up to the sound of the hills
while infants in tombs
grow up to the sound of the waves

A supernova shines only when it self-destructs
by which new stars arise
I wonder who and who else I was
far away
        far far away

Without a sound

resin buried underground is turning into amber
while above the first snow is falling

*

I came
from the Lion
You came
from the Archer

We're only guests in this world; let's linger a while then depart

*

That steep alleyway!
where
people live happily
True happiness in homes of the poor!

*

Along the path
a roebuck
is quietly contemplating the moon in a stream

What is this world?

Here's a butterfly fluttering by
and there's a spider's web

*

In the old days a poet once said
our nation is destroyed
yet the mountains and rivers survive

Today's poet says
the mountains and rivers are destroyed
yet our nation survives

Tomorrow's poet will say
the mountains and rivers are destroyed
our nation is destroyed and Alas!
you and I are completely destroyed

In every window of the primary school
the setting sun is glowing

each golden window a very god

*

The beak of a chick pecking at feed
My studies too are far from complete

*

A father in baggy pants
climbing up a footbridge
carrying his son's lunchbox

near a primary school in a town of fifty thousand inhabitants

Outside the window it looks freezing cold with not a breath of wind
In front of me
two orchids bloom side by side

The Chinese word for patience hangs on the opposite wall
in calligraphy by the patriot-martyr An Jung-gun

*

Comma
period
after forty-five sloppy years of mine
thank you

I promise never to put you to shame again

The Sioux have no word for good-bye
The moon will rise again tomorrow night
one day after the full moon
the sixteenth day's moon

*

Grandmother used to say
"Do the most trivial tasks,
even threading
a needle, with all your might"

But nowadays I can't see a needle's eye

*

When a mother calls her chicks
and chicks call their mother
their busy birdsong

is heard by other birds on the hillside opposite

Look at the nose of a baby rabbit
look at the tail of a dog—
that's the kind of world I'm living in

*

Near the bird tracks in the snow
I searched for the spirit of my sister
Sonhwa . . .
Sonhwa . . .
Sonhwa!

How can one flower ever be alone?
Look, over there
in that dry river bed
so very homely
that might be your love

*

A madhouse is a marvelous place—
I'm an emperor
I'm a major general
I'm the UN Secretary General
I'm pop singer Park Hun
I'm God
I'm Miss Korea
I'm the movie star Kim Bo-gil
One madhouse is annex to another madhouse

A cat's a degenerate beast of prey
A dog's a degenerate beast of prey
I'm a degenerate beast of prey

We've come so far from primitive times
today all we've got left
is petty guile

*

When the stalls were closing last market day
I suddenly glimpsed
Samman's ma who died last year
I suppose she came back to do some shopping

A peninsula is a place visitors come to
A peninsula is a place visitors leave again

Is that why there are so many bars
in the southern half of the Korean peninsula?

Some three million eight hundred thousand of them

We were flying over the Yenisei River
in the Western Siberian lowland
or was it the Ob River
near Doborsk perhaps?
or near Omsk?
A glint of sunlight reflected in a window down below
came flying up to where I sat
inside a window ten thousand meters up

It was all over in three seconds

Then we were passing over the Urals

"Bye!"
My greeting was belated as usual
That powerful sunbeam had already vanished

       *

                Don't!
                Don't!
                The sheath spent the whole night
                restraining the knife
                How still the sheath and the knife inside

A cock crows at Donghyun's
A cock crows at Yongsik's
A cock crows at Sunnam's
A cock crows at Gumchol's
Gumchol's grandpa has stopped breathing

*

Dogs are barking in villages high and low
Will this evening's thief
be called Kim or Park?

A homicidal thief with twelve prior convictions
was once a three-year-old kid—
and mad King Yonsan, who did crazy things stark naked
was once a four-year-old kid
and a cute one-year-old, too

*

Tell me, gong, hanging up there:
what youthful wildness, what festivals are you dreaming of?

*

Mother hen outside the egg
baby chick inside the egg—
the two are really one single body

I gazed blankly
at fields where people were working
Grandfather's tomb
where he was buried after working a lifetime
gazed blankly back

I pulled my hands out of my pockets

    *

What can I do?
Peach blossom petals
have been drifting all day long into the empty house

That flower
seen as I went down
—as I was coming up
I couldn't see it

ko Un

*

In the juvenile reformatory
his hands get exercise
his arms get exercise every day
They mustn't get stiff
Then once he's out
he'll be able to pick pockets again!

*

In the spring breeze
what agitation
in this valley
and that
I can't control my feelings
ah, those she-flowers and he-flowers

Ox-head's disappeared?
Horse-head's appeared?
All those founders of Buddhist sects
said useless things all their lives

*

Thirty years ago
a starving woman saw
a thousand sacks of rice in a mirage

*

Why is the sky so open?

I'm quite alone

The beetle husk caught in the spider's web
is riding a swing in the chill breeze
It must be very very bored

        *

             Get yourself a friend
             come to know a foe
             Get yourself a foe
             come to know a friend

             What kind of a game is this?

               *

                     Omar Khayyám—
                     on your sixty-seventh birthday
                     you dreamed of an observatory

                     Your only wealth was earthly wine
                     and all the stars in the sky

                     The child kept emerging within the old man . . .

A thousand drops
hanging from a dead branch

The rain did not fall for nothing

       *

Up on the hill
a cow stnds in the rain

Down below under the eaves
I wait for the rain to stop

For some time after, we avoid each other's eyes

One day
there was no one I could ask the way
so I set off
where a long pine branch was pointing

and found that the right direction

*

Ko Un

At times I feel I am suffocating
Is there nothing but this world?
At best
is there nothing but the other world?

*

The sleeping faces
under the prison cell's 60-watt bulb

were all children that had once been in my womb

Across the sandy shore
with never a word
into the sea
with never a word
the baby turtle began its long journey

   *

      In the March sunshine
      woosh
         woosh
      with gaping mouths

      flower buds are opening

Why shouldn't there be times when you long for another life?
The open eyes of that dead carp

*

I live, not knowing what I'll be tomorrow

One evening when I was rather drunk
lightning flashed
and disclosed me to the world

*

The day is coming when humans won't have mothers

At the zoo
I linger watching
a mother orangutan and her baby

Dog and pig
and cock
and hen and goose
and cat
and nine chicks
all day long
Relations neither good
nor bad

Chicken shit here and there in the yard
—Are they bored?

*

Over the hill
pretty Suni's family barley field—
oh, to turn into a skylark and go soaring aloft

New Year's Day, one old beggar
goes all round the village

Aren't these the so-called Good Old Days?

*

Everything outside my home
is my teacher

Master Horse Shit
Master Cow Shit

Master Children's Freckles

I really wonder
Time after time I've been buried
Therefore
I am many tombs

Yet still I've kept bragging "Here I am"

*

There has to be more energy for loving
than energy for hating
Here in this world,
and in the other world too,
there is a morning, evening, night worth living

I light a lamp in solitude

One spring night, the sound of a child weeping
One autumn night, the sound of laundry being pounded
This
was a place where people were really alive

As I passed the field fertilized with their shit
involuntarily I bowed my head

*

Perpetual movement!
Endless change!
You are all there is left to be enlightened about

Ah, ten years of study—all for nothing

*

We touch trees with our hands
We tread grass with our feet
So in that case
people are neighbors of trees, neighbors of grass!

I hate books
I hate the louts who read books
thanks to them
the mind is dead

Like a canteen with piles of empty rice bowls, like an empty pig sty

*

During the past seventy years
I have lived with a host of geniuses
If I had been a genius
I would not have known that happiness

Friedrich Wilhelm Nietzsche!
Amadeus!
Li Ho!
And the anonymous geniuses of old Korea!

From across the river
the sound of a bell reached the two of us
for us to listen to together
The sound of a bell reached us

We had decided to part
but then we decided not to part

                    *

                    I reckon it's the warmest expression of consolation
                    in the world:
                    the sound of the snow clustered
                    on green pine branches
                    sliding down

                              *

                                        Longing to explode once more
                                        Longing to be a sea of fire

                                        Paeknok Lake in the crater of Halla Mountain

Maybe I was in Chinburyong in Kangwon Province
Is there anything anywhere in the world
to match a snowy landscape?

Spring days
autumn colors
the indigo East Sea—
they all make us feel rather sad

*

At the foot of a hill where children are playing
a dainty stream babbles
It does not realize that very soon
it will be the sea

The early dawn sky was hazy
The pearly pebbles on the eastern sea shore slept on
A long dream
I don't even realize the sun's rising

*

The full moon steals through the clouds
Taken by surprise the thief runs off
The dogs bark in surprise

*

Snow softly sprinkles
the exposed flesh
of fresh newly chopped firewood

strangers to each other

The house by the roadside
has no yard
no fence
Where's that other shoe?

*

There are twelve new-born chicks in the yard
following their mother

Needless to say a kîte hangs far above

*

Go to Somalia
and look at your capîtalism
look at your socialism
Look in the eyes of ſtarving children

The dog in its wretched kennel
does not so much as glance at palaces
or rich mansions

    *

Beneath the low horizon at Sonyu Island in Kogun-san
the sun sets with a splash

We should not be unthinkingly sad

    *

Let those who have parted company
go
to the winter sea
Let those who once loved intensely
go
rather than those who love intensely now

That business tycoon's tremendous mansion—
the despair of beggars
the hope of burglars

*

At 1:30 A.M.
across the road in Apartment Block 16
six lights were still burning
One went out

Then another

*

Somewhere near Soyang Lake
one becomes two
somehow
One becomes three
the lake
and you and I

64

At the lakeside
I shouted your name
Behind the vanishing echo
You . . .
                Where are you
                            Where are

                *

                        Borne along on a rushing stream
                        willow seeds
                        touching land
                        burst open

                        Try starting just like that

Creatures
living between river and sea
eels
king crabs
you really study hard

                    *

                              Guests for a thousand years—
                              a dragon-fly perching on a water-lily
                              and I

                         *

                              Cobweb drenched all day long by monsoon rain
                              you too are enduring great trials

As I learned
from the wind
my nirvana is a wandering nirvana
I've also learned much from such things as
clouds
rain
ditch-water

I'm an always wandering student

     *

Last night
in a dream I was clinging to far-off Saturn's rings
Hey, little puppy
what did you dream?

As I emerged
from a Chinese restaurant in Crete
my foot slipped
The sea tilted
then
Poseidon rose majestic from the sea and sank again

*

Quite true

Shakyamuni
crossed the sea from India
and once here
became a different
Shakyamuni

So wonderful—we all become something different

*

All night long in the freshly planted paddy-field
a team of a thousand frogs has been at work

No greed can equal freedom from greed
Apart from that
the petty desires
of all you ordinary folk
are
the truth existing between this world and the other

So: cheers!

*

What labor is there
to equal nature?

Today
I sowed seeds in a scrap of field
Nature will germinate them, raising them well

How really selfish people can be

All things
sing and speak
birds sing in birdsong
rocks speak in silence
And me?

All my babbling is just so much nonsense

*

So long as swallows come flying back
I have a reason to live
So long as the sea
those swallows cross
has a southern shore
there's a reason for waiting for tomorrow

I have a reason for longing for you.

Ko Un

Tomorrow I'm going to meet
Lee Dong-Sun from Taegu
at a cafe in Insa-dong in Seoul

Tomorrow I'll go to the post office and mail a letter
then in the evening I'll continue to read a book about Mongolian culture

Tomorrow I'll be lazier than today

How happy all those plans
plain as a cold cabbage-patch

Yet
tomorrow is already today

At the market in Ansong
people buying
people selling
people who were sick
but got up again yesterday or the day before

even people who don't know each other get acquainted

*

I venerate people who travel far
from their birth place
their native land

Only a life that founds something new
does not imitate other lives

like the first king of the first Korean kingdom, Ko Jumong at twenty

In the rain the grass is dancing
In the rain the stones are sleeping

*

Truly, lies are impossible
On the last night of the month
one waning moon shines

*

Moonlit night reveals your lungs and everything
Even the tombs are shifting slightly

In a remote mountain valley
a startled pheasant flies off squawking
Hey!
You think you alone are startled?
I was startled too

*

In the Outer Diamond Mountains I could not write a poem
In the Inner Diamond Mountains I could not write a poem
My empty body was full of truth

*

To a poor fellow who has
no stone-hard horse
no cast-iron cow
not even a black pig

what point would there be in talking about Buddha?

Compassion is
tenderness of heart

You say the Tao is possible
without tenderness?

With that sort of Tao, what petty larceny do you intend?

       *

                  Humans show their humanity
                  by talking

                  Hey, you there in the bow-tie!
                  Don't nod off

                  Say something: what-
                  ever

The first raindrop
wakes
a magnolia leaf
then
this leaf
then that

                    *

                              Sound of raindrops falling from eaves
                              I
                              and a spider are speechless half the day

                                        *

                                                  Once ghosts have been expelled
                                                  sheer boredom
                                                  Head priest at Kaya Mountain Temple
                                                  don't say too quickly
                                                  that a flower is blooming in the fire

                                                  What else will you do
                                                  when a butterfly flies in?

Once you have cracked all 1700 koans
there will still be a boat
on the water
In the sky there will still be clouds

*

I had no thought
of hearing thunder when it sounded

I'd had no visitors for a long while

No need to know its whereabouts

A small spring in a mountain ravine
is like a sister
a younger sister
like a long lost younger sister
now found again

*

At early dawn
the sound of the first cock crowing

I suppose they can hear it in that room too?

Why
   Why
      Why
A bright day
A five-year-old was busy with questions

Surely that child knows
that without those Why's
everything would be pointless

     *

It is said that nothing can become new
unless it first turns to ashes
For a whole decade
my misfortune was not having turned to ashes

Burning a mound of dead leaves in late autumn I want to weep

There is a mountain . . .
Late in a good-for-nothing life
at least I have been something for a mountain

*

Why is "now" a millennium's end
a millennium's beginning?
Now on the spot
I sober up

I get up from where I've been drinking

A line of ants
is crossing a road
perhaps so that we can realize
today
and tomorrow
and the day after
little by little
that this world does not belong
only to humanity

At noontime hot as a charcoal fire, the cuckoo has stopped calling

      *

Let's not talk only of Siberia's severe cold
In Siberia's blazing summer heat
the bones of a rotting carp shine white

You might well call it the paradox of paradoxes
Truly I tell you
Ask poor people about today
Ask poor countries about tomorrow
Ask Native Americans
or Somalian women
about the new century
Not rich Americans

*

At the spot where last summer a tank went past
this autumn a wild chrysanthemum blossomed

KO Un

I long to go to a place fragrant with the smell
of water on spring evenings like a mother, like a sister,
to go to the sea off Cholla with its many islands

       *

We can never again speed
on four legs
over those plains
and ridges where the mist has cleared

Ah, the curse of *homo erectus*

       *

Earthworm!
How is it you live so long, stretching and shrinking
without even one exquisite song

Humility!
A boat entering harbor
Arrogance!
A boat leaving harbor

*

Heavy snow is falling
Heavy snow is falling
Everything is childlike

*

Beside the maple
stands a dogwood
Beside the dogwood
stands an oak
And beside the oak
stands my wife

The mother cow is lowing
the calf is lowing

Humans only imitate their ancient love

                    *

                    Up the hilltop slope of the slum
                    a man walked through the falling sleet
                    A dog came dashing out

                    Just look at that dog's tail!

                    *

                              The path had survived from the old days
                              Suddenly between two poplars
                              my dead brother was standing
                              It was a twilight path

In the Korean peninsula there's buried more longing than coal
Kith and kin scattered 55–60 years ago
a cast-iron DMZ lies between them
to the south of which
to the north of which
longing is everyone's full-time job

Korean peninsula! surrounded by longing on all three sides

If it's all a matter of morning dew
there is nothing more to be hoped for
If it's a matter of morning dew
hanging glistening in spiders' webs
there's nothing more to be done

Dear young friends
it's alright to do nothing all the clear bright day

                    *

                         Light across the river

                         No one asked
                         No one answered

Someone walking is most beautiful
People
    meeting and walking together, that's most beautiful
The sky is full of fluffy clouds

The top is spinning
Yesterday the poet Midang departed
today old Oh from next door departed
How can death concern only one or two?
The child's top is surrounded by every kind of death

      *

I lost my way
On and on nothing but sand
it was the Gobi Desert
Buried bones emerged from the sand—
Good to see you!

Whereabouts
will my bones
become a path for a future world?

My heart pounded—an oasis loomed ahead

Look at the flowers
A whore enjoys them
Look at the flowers
Fourteen-year-old Sonhui enjoys them too

*

New as a debt repaid today
New as a tomb dug today
How often does it happen?
There are lives that start anew like this
Over there
A butterfly—maybe one maybe two

Why
shouldn't there be times when you long to gaze straight into the sun
until you're completely blind?
While I said I loved you I loved myself
While I said I loved my neighbors
While I said I loved the world I simply loved myself

Frogs are croaking in the patch of weeds in the ditch

*

House left empty while they earn money
The sound of a distant bell
reaches it
A dog hears
The blue sky looks down silently

Remorse! Without it, what truth can there be?
Mid-November
Someone is standing by the sea at Taebu Island
at low tide
Scraps of trash drift by

*

On the evening of Buddha's birthday
I saw her under the lamps
Boldly
I saw her previous lives
and as she walked round a pagoda she saw me

*

As we flew over Kaema Plateau in North Korea
I felt guilty toward the friend I was with
Actually
I prayed the plane might fall
I don't know why
That plateau in the clouds
was so utterly my other world

Last night, several of you were crying
At dawn, I realize
hey, you're alone!
Little insect
I'm awake so I'm your comrade

Seoul Prison Block 5 Cell 1

*

Next time I really must wear a cotton skirt
I must walk quickly down Grandma's path
Mother's path
balancing a basket on my head
with food for the workers in the fields

After 29 years, I visited the fields of my native village
and saw them there

A warship moves through the sea
near Paekryong Island in the Yellow Sea
Not one seagull's in sight
The sea
looks as if someone has disappeared in it
I'm carrying an empty *soju* bottle

Translators' Afterword

Flowers blossom to be enjoyed.

That simple.

So too is it with these pages. Only to appreciate them a bit more fully, consideration from some diverse angles might be useful, about their contexts, trajectories, and certainly their most remarkable author, Ko Un (say "goh eun").

No treatise. No program. Nothing formal. Rather, as if we were listening to the sounds of waves, whose persistence gesture toward their influences and source.

Ko Un is a master of the short poem. Within this compact format, we can see his talent ranging across many themes and styles, lyric, hermetic, realist, populist, pastoral, historical, dissident, spiritual, prophetic, etc.

A quick survey shows some poems here as being about big things. Lightning, and volcanoes. Genius, and ancient kings. Predominant, though, is the small. Breezes, and streams. Minnows, and bugs.

Sometimes, the diminutive is used to evoke the limpid, the evanescent, the poignant. The sound of snow falling from pine branches.

In the margins of the manuscript, we noted a recurrence of images of transformation and renewal. Seeds of particular plants. Clay baking in a kiln. A mineral becoming a jewel in the matrix of the earth. The chicken and the egg.

Then there's the Butterfly Effect, in which something as simple as the flapping of a butterfly's wings in the Amazon can affect the weather in Texas. We can witness similar elegant complexities upon the woven wood fiber of these pages. Through the lens of a poet naturalist, what might seem a simple *thing* becomes a pattern in a web of relationship. Process, rather than a product.

There's an affinity here, too, for the ordinary. Cows and dogs. And sympathy for the underdog. Beggars and burglars.

The abbreviated measure of these poems is apt for today's hurried literacy. At play here is a minimalism that's anything but sterile reductionism. Rather this vigorous view gets at the light within each thing (the light, and the dark); as it is. Just so.

If such be minimalism, its reach is global.

In the poet's amplitude and delicacy, some readers might detect a cultural influence of China's gift for synthesis and suggestion. Others might remark that their artifice seems Japanese. Yet, really, at bottom, they're very Korean.

Even though we've translated these poems into English, their Koreanness still clings to them the way the roots of transplanted vegetation still carry native earth. Before looking at this Koreanness in any depth, however, a caveat would be proper: there's no intention here of even remotely suggesting anything resembling the least iota of Orientalism. Nevertheless, to appreciate universality is to appreciate its grounding in a particular soil. Fortunately, both dimensions—the particular and the universal, the transcendent and the historical—are always intertwined; interpenetrating.

At the 2003 conference, "Ko Un's Poetic World," at Stockholm University, Jesper R. Matsumoto Mulbjerg typified Ko Un the poet as: "very much Korean—very much a human being."

From 1895 to 1945 Korea was erased from maps of the world. Ko Un was born into this dark period, when Korea was under Japanese colonial rule, a time when the Korean language and writing system were forbidden; utterly suppressed. Like everyone else, he was forced to transform his own name into a Japanese one. At primary school, all his classes were conducted in Japanese. Still, Ko Un managed to learn Korean, from a neighbor's farmhand, in secret.

Korea's indigenous language is classified as a branch of the Altaic family, which had spread across the north and central Asian steppes to become root for Japanese, Manchurian, Mongolian, and Turkish; it also shows traces of the Ural family, related to Finnish and Hungarian. Eventually, Chinese was used as the writing system, and today nearly half of the Korean vocabulary is composed of Chinese words. But in the 15th century Korean King Sejong declared using Chinese characters (*hanja*) "too complicated, imperfect, and inconvenient a system for Koreans to use in freely expressing their own ideas and thinking."

The outcome, *hankul*, is arguably the most efficient system ever devised in the history of writing; hailed by linguistics scholar Geoffrey Sampson as "one of the great intellectual achievements of humankind." Consonants are a graphic representation of how sounds are articulated in the mouth: ㅅ = a tooth, used to pronounce "s"; ㄱ = the tongue at the back of the throat, used to pronounce "k"; ㄴ = the tongue at the front of the mouth, used to pronounce "n."

Unveiling the national writing system to his people in 1446, King Sejong noted that hankul is capable of recording music and song (!), " . . . and can even describe the sound of the wind, the chirp of birds, the cawing of crows, and the barking of dogs."

With a national writing system created in the 15th century came new forms of expression, such as the three-line sijo. Sijo is more subjective compared to the objectivist haiku. Sijo freely uses the first-person singular "I," the human amidst the earthly and the heavenly. We can hear a resonance in our own heart, relating a poem's universals to the personal.

And sijo was the first national vernacular poetry. The vernacular, in general, grew in importance to Korean poetics. A reader can approach much Korean poetry as if it weren't even written at all, but spoken thought.

Sijo and haiku, proverbs and riddles, epigrams and brief poems, all enlist us in their own creation. Our participation is part of the performance; our interpretation becomes part of the poetry.

With so much left out, we're invited to fill in the blank. Complete the circle. Or discover the vanishing point of the line off at the edge of the horizon, between the heavens and earth, a point that's also smack dab in the heart of the heart.

In 1952, after witnessing the horrors of the Korean War, Ko Un entered a Buddhist monastery. He attained priesthood before returning to secular life in 1962. Naturally, Ko Un's brief poems are often compared to Buddhist meditation.

One example is found in the practice of using a seemingly illogical word, phrase, or sentence, inviting the practitioner to break free of the prison of language, and its prison guards of discursive logic. To perceive reality directly.

There's a dynamic at play here between the familiar and the totally unfamiliar, between the rational and the intuitive, and from this tension can arise deep creative vitality.

Other times, poetry might occur when, as Ko Un writes, "a practitioner experiences a sudden flash of insight or wisdom. The resultant joy emerges as a poetic gleam, and results in a few lines of poetry, in which someone denying writing uses a few letters to express an inner peak of experience."

Ko Un's spiritual training became ingrained the way a concert pianist doesn't think about the notes being played. So too might the reader find his or her own childlike intuition cracking the puzzling nut of some of these poems. And certain poems might seem espe-cially indicative of stages of their own journey's peaks and valleys.

This kind of artless art is kin to ink-brush calligraphy, springing forth from a quiet zone of long, deep concentration, as you can see in the dozen wordless poems gracing these pages.

And the typically terse nature of East Asian language is an elemental measure. As of breath. Breath, hinge of body and mind. Constant companion, a friendly reminder of our true home, in the here and in the now.

Of course, there's no such thing as Korean breath, Korean truth. Still we can speak of particulars of Korean culture, manifest in Ko Un's poetry: rustic unpretentiousness, earthiness, informality, spontaneity, easy humor, understated simplicity, exhilarating vigor, dynamic design.

Two qualities fundamental to contemporary Korean sensibility are found here: *han,* bitter sorrow, and *heung,* joyful mirth. Sharing our tears—and the light in darkness.

Koreans are survivors. With night, think not of an ending, but return of light. Thus do Koreans "see."

These poems are short, not small. Brief, as a heartbeat. Momentary as the turning of a page.

Poetry is your own encounter with these pages, your being present with their spell.

You are cordially invited
to celebrate the bigness of being,
the mystery of the holy ordinary,
the flowers of a moment.

Acknowledgments

The poet and translators wish to thank the Lannan Foundation for their indespensible support of the translation and publication of this book, the Korean Literature Translation Institute, and Professor Lee Sang-hwa for her close review of the manuscript. Thanks are owed as well to the editors of the following publications in which some of these translations first appeared: *BuddhaDharma: The Practitioner's Quarterly*; *The Nation; New College Review; The New Yorker; Turning Wheel: The Journal of Socially Engaged Buddhism; Two Lines: A Journal of Translation*; and *World Literature Today*. Additional thanks to Joe Flower, Robert Hass, Aeju Lee, Kate Miles Melville, Erin Noteboom, and Kim Shuck.

About the Author

Ko Un was born in 1933 in Kunsan, Korea, and grew up during the Japanese Occupation. After witnessing the Korean War, he became a Buddhist monk in 1952. He walked all over war-ravaged Korea as a mendicant, mastered meditation, and helped found the first national Korean Buddhist newspaper, where his first poems were published.

Returning to secular life in the early 1960s, already an established poet, he lived for several years on Jeju Island before returning to Seoul. These were dark years of nihilism and despair, until he heard of young garment-worker Jeon Tae-il's self-immolation to protest the government's failure to implement and enforce its promised labor laws. Ko Un soon became a familiar figure at demonstrations and protests against the military dictatorship, and organized a number of pro-democracy associations. He and fellow-protesters were often arrested, beaten; some, tortured and killed.

Following the assassination in 1979 of military dictator Park Jung-Hee, another general staged a coup in 1980 and Ko Un, Kim Dae-Jung, and hundreds of others were rounded up, thrown into prison, and sentenced to death or given arbitrary sentences in courts-martial. The long months alone in a tiny, darkened cell—his hearing virtually destroyed by police beatings, unsure if he would emerge alive—wrought yet another radical change in Ko Un's life.

Upon his release, he married Lee Sang-hwa in 1983, moved to a house in the countryside where they raised a daughter, and he wrote undisturbed. *Flowers of a Moment* appeared in April 2001, one year before publication of his complete works to date, 38 volumes gathering over 125 titles (poetry, essays, fiction, drama, and translations). In the past decade, portions of this vast opus have been translated into every major language, and he has been invited to read his work in many countries. Homepage: http://www.koun.co.kr

About the Translators

Brother Anthony was born in Britain in 1942. He studied at Queen's College, Oxford University, before joining the Community of Taizé (France) in 1969. He lived in the Philippines from 1977 to 1980, then moved to Korea, where he became a naturalized citizen in 1994. He is a professor in the English Department of Sogang University, Seoul. His published translations of Korean literature include Ko Un's *The Sound of My Waves*, *Ten Thousand Lives*, *Little Pilgrim*, *Beyond Self*, and *Songs for Tomorrow*. He has also published translations of poems by Ku Sang, Midang, Ch'ŏn Sang-Pyŏng, Kim Su-Yŏng, Shin Kyŏng-Nim, Lee Si-Yŏng, and Kim Kwang-Kyu, et al., and fiction by Yi Mun-Yol among others—some 20 volumes so far. Homepage: http://anthony/sogang.ac.kr

Young-moo Kim was born in 1944 in Paju, near Seoul. After graduating from Seoul National University, he received his Ph.D. from SUNY at Stony Brook and became a Professor in the Department of English Language and Literature at Seoul National University. He and Brother Anthony collaborated in translating Ko Un and several other Korean poets' works into English. He began to write his own poems in 1991 and has published three volumes. His last collection, *Virtual Reality*, which centered on his struggle with cancer, received the 2001 Paeksŏk Award. He died on November 26, 2001.

Gary Gach was born in 1947 in Los Angeles and received a B.A. from SFSU in 1970. Honored with an American Book Award for his anthology *What Book!?: Buddha Poems from Beat to Hiphop*, he is also author of *The Complete Idiot's Guide to Buddhism* (second edition), *Preparing the Ground: Poems 1960–70*, *Writers.Net*, and several other titles. With C. H. Kwock, he has translated poetry from all the dynasties of China. A San Francisco Bay-swimmer, he teaches at Book Passage University, San Francisco Zen Center, and Stanford Continuing Studies. Homepage: http://word.to

The Lannan Translations Selection Series

Ljuba Merlina Bortolani, *The Siege*

Olga Orozco, *Engravings Torn from Insomnia*

Gérard Martin, *The Hiddenness of the World*

Fadhil Al-Azzawi, *Miracle Maker*

Sándor Csoóri, *Before and After the Fall: New Poems*

Francisca Aguirre, *Ithaca*

Jean-Michel Maulpoix, *A Matter of Blue*

Willow, Wine, Mirror, Moon: Women's Poems from Tang China

Felípe Benítez Reyes, *Probable Lives*

Ko Un, *Flowers of a Moment*

For more on the Lannan Translations Selection Series
visit our Web site:
www.boaeditions.org